My
FUTURE
CAREER

Working in

Engineering

Margaret McAlpine

GARETH**STEVENS**
GS
PUBLISHING
A WRC Media Company

Please visit our web site at: **www.garethstevens.com**
For a free color catalog describing Gareth Stevens Publishing's
list of high-quality books and multimedia programs, call
1-800-542-2595 (USA) or 1-800-387-3178 (Canada).
Gareth Stevens Publishing's fax: (414) 332-3567.

Library of Congress Cataloging-in-Publication Data

McAlpine, Margaret.
     Working in engineering / Margaret McAlpine.
        p. cm. — (My future career)
     Includes bibliographical references and index.
     ISBN 0-8368-4773-3 (lib. bdg.)
     1. Engineering—Vocational guidance. I. Title. II. Series.
     TA157.M3418   2005
     620'.0023—dc22   2005042458

This edition first published in 2006 by
Gareth Stevens Publishing
A WRC Media Company
330 West Olive Street, Suite 100
Milwaukee, Wisconsin 53212 USA

This U.S. edition copyright © 2006 by Gareth Stevens, Inc. Original
edition copyright © 2004 by Hodder Wayland. First published in 2005
by Hodder Wayland, an imprint of Hodder Children's Books.

Editor: Dorothy L. Gibbs
Inside design: Peta Morey
Cover design: Melissa Valuch

Picture Credits
Angela Hampton Family Life Picture Library 46, 50. **Corbis:** Roger Ball 36,
38, 58; Peter Barrett 55; Bettmann Archives 53; Steve Crise 22; George Disario 43;
FK Photo 41; Freelance Consulting Services Pty, Inc. 20; Stephen Frink 44; Rick Gayle
27 (bottom); Philip Gould 42; Brownie Harris 8, 40, 56, 59; Eric Hausman 52; Ralf-
Finn Hestoft 6; Ted Horowitz 32, 39; Bob Krist 54; Lester Lefkowitz 13, 16, 29;
Lucidio Studio, Inc. 15; John Madere 35 (top); Tom and Dee McCarthy 12; Jean
Miele 17; Charles O'Rear 11, 31; Gabe Palmer 37; Roger Ressmeyer 9, 14, 28, 47;
Reuters 27 (top); Jeffrey L. Rotman 49; Bob Rowan/Progressive Image 57; Pete
Saloutos 5; M. L. Sinibaldi 33; Richard Hamilton Smith 45; Paul A. Souders 4;
Paul Steel 23; Keren Su 25; Jim Sugar 7; William Taufic 18, 19, 21; Bill Varie 10,
30. **Corbis Sygma:** Hekimian Julien 48; Jacques Langevin 24; Orban Theirry 35
(bottom). **Getty Images:** cover. **Science Photo Library:** Colin Cuthbert 51.
Note: Photographs illustrating "A day in the life of . . ." pages are posed by models.

Gareth Stevens Publishing thanks the following individuals and organizations
for their professional assistance: Christopher J. Italiano, B.A.E.M.; Russell J. Fisher,
Ch.E., President, Fisher Composite Technologies, LLC; Kurt E. Feuerstein, P.E.,
Senior Transportation Engineer; Mike Prem, B.S.E.E.; Robert Way, Product Engineer,
Galway Pumps; Tim Graul, N.A., Tim Graul marine design; and Matthew Burdick,
Mechanical Engineer.

Printed in China

1 2 3 4 5 6 7 8 9 09 08 07 06 05

Contents

Words that appear in the text in **bold**
type are defined in the glossary.

Aerospace Engineer

What is an aerospace engineer?

Aerospace engineers make things fly. They plan, design, build, test, and maintain everything from **airframes** to **flight control systems** on all types of aircraft, including passenger planes, fighter jets, helicopters, satellites, rockets, and the Space Shuttle, and they make sure that all parts of aircraft function correctly and safely.

Aeronautical engineers have studied the flight patterns of birds to help create and improve aircraft designs.

Aerospace engineering is a combination of two fields of engineering: aeronautical and astronautical. Aeronautical engineers specialize in designing and manufacturing aircraft that fly within the atmosphere, which is the band of gases surrounding Earth, while astronautical engineers specialize in vehicles that operate outside the atmosphere, including satellites, rockets, and unmanned spacecraft.

Aerospace engineers work in other industries, too. In the **automotive** industry, they help make the interiors of cars and trucks quieter and the exteriors less resistant to wind. In boat and ship manufacturing, they design vessels that move easily through water.

Flight "Patterns"

Humans have been fascinated by the idea of flight for a very long time. In 1486, Leonardo da Vinci, who was an engineer as well as an artist and sculptor, began studying birds to find out how they flew. Da Vinci went on to design a number of different flying machines based on his research, but none of his designs was successfully constructed.

Americans Wilbur and Orville Wright were two of the world's most famous aeronautical engineers. In 1903, the Wright brothers carried out the first successful powered flight in a heavier-than-air machine with a pilot on board. Later, the Wright brothers set up an aircraft factory, which marked the beginning of the aeronautical industry.

Today, air travel is the best way to cross the world quickly and safely.

Since the Wright brothers, all successful airplanes have incorporated the basic design elements of the brothers' early aircraft, known as Wright Flyers. The way the Wright brothers worked set the pattern for research and development in the aerospace industry. They carried out carefully planned tests and collected data, which they examined, analyzed, and then used to make changes in their designs.

Main responsibilities of an aerospace engineer

All aerospace engineers need to have a thorough understanding of physics, **aerodynamics**, **propulsion**, and materials. Beyond that, most aerospace engineers specialize in particular areas of work. The main areas of work in the aircraft industry are research and development, aircraft design, model making, aircraft production, and aircraft maintenance.

- Research and development engineers create ideas for new aircraft and solve problems and identify improvements for existing aircraft. All aircraft operate in a wide variety of conditions caused by weather and **altitude**. Engineers in research and development have to make sure that aircraft operate safely and reliably in all possible conditions. These engineers also investigate new and improved technologies by modifying and testing existing products.
- Design engineers develop the plans for aircraft and improvements created by research and development teams. They work to create products that are safe,

Some aerospace and aeronautical engineers are responsible for supervising the maintenance of aircraft and making sure the aircraft are safe to fly. Routine maintenance tasks are usually performed by specially trained mechanics.

Good Points and Bad Points

"Supervising the maintenance side of the aerospace industry is a great job. I like to feel I'm using my knowledge and qualifications in a practical way."

"My job involves a high level of responsibility, and I cannot afford to make a mistake, so the work can be very stressful."

dependable, easily manufactured and maintained, economical, and good for the environment and that use fuel and other resources efficiently.

- Many aerospace engineers make and test models of aircraft to help ensure that the aircraft will operate as they were designed to. By working on models, engineers can identify problems more quickly and economically than by working on full-size aircraft.

- Production engineers work on the construction of aircraft. Engineers who work in aircraft factories oversee manufacturing procedures and production workers to make sure that workmanship meets high standards.

- Maintenance engineers thoroughly check all aircraft on a regular basis to ensure safe operation. Routine maintenance identifies both structural and mechanical problems and weaknesses before they become a danger to passengers and crew. An aerospace engineer is usually in charge of a team of technicians, mechanics, and airframe specialists who carry out the maintenance tasks.

Models such as these provide an efficient way to test a new aircraft design's performance before building a much more expensive full-size version.

Main qualifications of an aerospace engineer

Knowledge of mathematics and science
Just as for most other fields of engineering, aerospace engineers need to have a strong and broad education in math, including algebra, geometry, calculus, and trigonometry, and science, especially biology, physics, and chemistry.

Creativity
Aerospace engineers are pushing back the boundaries of science all the time. They need to think creatively and use their imaginations to visualize the flight needs and possibilities of the future.

An eye for detail
The work of aerospace engineers is usually very precise, and every detail of a project is extremely important.

Awareness of safety needs
Because accidents in the air are always disastrous, safety is a major issue in air travel. A passenger who feels unsafe on an airplane will choose another form of transportation for future travel. Aeronautical engineers need to make sure that aircraft designs and workmanship meet the highest possible safety standards.

To work on a jet engine, an aeronautical engineer needs to have a very high level of technical skill and knowledge.

Computer skills
Especially in the areas of design, development, and testing, engineering jobs depend on the use of computers and specialized **software**.

Designing aircraft that can cope with the difficulties of space travel is a tremendous challenge for aerospace engineers.

fact file

Aerospace engineering requires, at least, a bachelor's degree in engineering. Many aerospace engineers start with a degree in mechanical engineering, then gain specialized knowledge and experience in the aerospace field by earning an advanced degree, working with experienced engineers, attending seminars and conferences, or completing an **internship**. Many jobs in aerospace engineering require professional licensing, which involves passing a state exam.

Teamwork

Aerospace projects can be enormous and involve a large number of people who all need to share ideas and work well together.

Communication skills

Aerospace engineers must speak and write clearly and effectively in communicating not only with other engineers but also with people in a wide range of non-engineering fields.

Language skills

Due to the enormous expense of developing and building aircraft and spacecraft, some countries have started working together and sharing the costs. As this type of cooperation becomes more common, engineers who speak foreign languages will be in great demand.

Martin Jones

Martin is employed at an aerospace manufacturing research center. He is currently working on an international project to develop a new type of passenger plane.

8:00 a.m. When I first arrive at work, I check my E-mail messages. An international project involves a lot of electronic communication.

8:30 a.m. I'm at my computer, which is where I spend about half of my time, mainly working with **CAD** and **simulation** software that allows me to create on-screen versions of projects. The expense of designing and producing a new type of aircraft is enormous, so before any part is manufactured, we need to make sure the work can be done efficiently, on time, and at an agreed upon price. Using computer simulations, I can predict whether a proposal from a company to do some of the work will meet our requirements at a price we can afford. The simulations also show any problems that might arise.

10:30 a.m. I look at proposals for manufacturing the wings of the aircraft. I have to enter figures and **data** from the proposals into the simulation program.

Safety is a major concern in air travel. This aerospace engineer is inspecting an airplane's brakes.

International projects, such as constructing this Airbus, bring together aerospace engineers from all over the world.

1:00 p.m. I spend many afternoons in the laboratory, building models, testing ideas, or performing experiments on my designs. Today, I'm making changes to a model based on some recent testing.

5:30 p.m. Back at my desk, I start working on a presentation for a meeting in a few weeks. Representatives from all of the countries involved in this project will be at the meeting. I have to talk to them about the proposals our research center has developed and explain how the proposals fit in with the project's expectations, budget, and timetable.

6:30 p.m. I finally turn off my computer and head to the gym for some much needed physical activity.

Chemical Engineer

What is a chemical engineer?

Chemical engineers use both chemistry and the principles of engineering to develop new products and to solve manufacturing problems that involve the use of chemicals. Every manufactured product, including fabric, paper, soap, and paint, to name only a few, involves chemical engineering at some point in the process.

Some chemical engineers work in laboratories.

Chemical engineering combines chemistry, physics, and math in practical ways. The engineers in this field process chemicals to make or alter materials, taking ideas from test tubes (lab research) to barrels (pilot runs), to **tank wagons** (production).

Processing begins by making small quantities of a substance, then carrying out tests to make sure the substance is safe. Engineers also test to make sure that the substance does what it is supposed to do.

The Wonders of Renewable Resources

With resources such as coal and oil becoming more limited — and more expensive, chemists are looking for help from renewable resources, such as vegetables! Scientists are experimenting with oils from corn, soybeans, and other vegies to replace petroleum in fuels of the future. And salad oil might just become the new plastic!

When a substance passes all tests, chemical engineers turn their attention to producing it in larger amounts. To prepare for mass production, they often use computer models to simulate the manufacturing process. Computer **simulation** helps engineers see what kinds of problems might develop when they produce the actual product.

Many chemical engineers work in factories and manufacturing plants.

Eventually, the product is manufactured. At this point, the responsibilities of a chemical engineer change. Now, the engineer must make sure that production runs smoothly, problems are solved, and the quality of the final product is satisfactory.

Main responsibilities of a chemical engineer

The work of chemical engineers involves a variety of roles and responsibilities. Some of the more general responsibilities include the following:

- meeting with clients and coworkers to determine the nature and requirements of a project
- using research, knowledge, and technical expertise to develop a plan that will achieve the project's goals
- preparing project budgets and time schedules
- defining the technical specifications of a project
- designing, developing, and supervising production and testing processes
- establishing and monitoring safety, quality control, and waste management procedures
- preparing progress reports for clients and coworkers

This chemical engineer is examining coal paste, which is a new type of fuel that is being developed as a clean alternative to traditional dry coal.

Good Points and Bad Points

"Chemical engineering offers great opportunities, including the chance to travel on the job, and for many years, this field has paid one of the highest starting salaries for workers with bachelor of science degrees."

"Chemical engineering projects often involve a great deal of money, and managing them can be both difficult and stressful."

While chemical engineers work in many different industries, they all use their skills and knowledge to improve Earth and the lives of its inhabitants.

- In the food industry, chemical engineers develop fertilizers that enrich the soil to help plants grow and to increase food production around the world.
- In the medical industry, chemical engineers help develop artificial organs and body parts. Artificial organs need to be made from materials that will not be rejected by the human body. Chemical engineers play an important part in discovering and producing these materials.
- In the field of materials engineering, **synthetics**, such as nylon, polyester, and plastics are results of chemical engineering research and development.
- In dealing with problems and issues related to the environment, the work of chemical engineers has provided ways to clean up and control waste and pollution. Unleaded gasoline, for example, is a result of chemical engineering.

The synthetic rubber used in athletic shoes was developed by chemical engineers. Most synthetic materials wear well and, usually, are inexpensive to produce.

Main qualifications of a chemical engineer

Good educational background

Knowledge of chemistry, math, and physics is the foundation of chemical engineering, and all need to have been studied at advanced levels.

A creative and open mind

Chemical engineers, especially those working in research, must be able to come up with ideas for both new and improved products and processes. Because they can never be absolutely certain about the results of their work, they must be able to discover and accept new theories and adapt their ideas accordingly.

Keeping detailed notes and up-to-date records is part of a chemical engineer's responsibility to protect the environment and public health.

Patience

Research in chemical engineering can go on for many years and may include long periods when very little progress is made. Chemical engineers must be patient and determined workers.

Organized work habits and attention to details

Both in research and production, chemical engineers must keep up-to-date records, noting details carefully and writing painstakingly accurate reports.

The use of computers for organizing and analyzing data is essential in chemical engineering.

fact file

A strong interest in chemistry and an aptitude for math and science are basic requirements for chemical engineering jobs. Most positions in this field require at least a bachelor's degree in chemical engineering. Many jobs call for professional engineers (PEs), who must also have four or five years of work experience and pass a state licensing exam.

Teamwork

Chemical engineers usually work in teams or with other professionals, not only sharing information but also relying on each other for information. To work effectively with others, chemical engineers must speak and write clearly and, above all, listen attentively.

Computer skills

Like so many other professions today, chemical engineering depends heavily on the use of computer technology and specialized **software** programs. Chemical engineers need to know, for example, how to gather and compile statistical **data** electronically and how to use computer hardware and software for data analysis and to control **automated** systems.

Amanda Ledbetter

Amanda works in a chemical plant that produces alcohol for use in cleaning products.

8:00 a.m.   When I arrive at the office, I check my E-mail messages, then meet with the senior chemical engineer about the day's work.

9:00 a.m.   I receive a phone call from the operations leader in our chemical plant, telling me that the finished product is "off spec," which means it doesn't match our customer's requirements.

I immediately rush to the plant and put on a hard hat and a pair of overalls. Then I go to work with the mechanical engineer, the control engineer, and the senior production operator to locate the source of the problem. To correct a processing error, we have to think on our feet and share our expertise until we figure out the cause of the problem. We have to work quickly so the customer can receive "on-spec" material on time.

We check different parts of the plant and examine the production process, including flow rates, temperatures, and pressures.

A chemical engineer's job may involve both desk work and work in a chemical plant or laboratory.

Whenever processing problems occur, workers in a chemical plant consult an engineer's plans to help them determine how to correct the problems.

10:30 a.m. We finally find the problem. It is connected with the raw materials being used.

11:00 a.m. Back at the office, I spend some time doing paperwork. Each month we produce statistics showing the levels of waste gases and liquids given off into the atmosphere. I use this information to prepare a report on waste materials, which must be sent to an external organization that makes sure our plant is not excessively polluting the environment.

12:30 p.m. I have lunch with some coworkers.

1:30 p.m. I participate in a **teleconference** with chemists at our main research center. We discuss how to run the plant in safer, more efficient, and more cost-effective ways.

4:00 p.m. I spend the last hour of the day at the plant, checking on the production process to make sure everything is running according to plan.

Civil Engineer

What is a civil engineer?

Civil engineers design, develop, and supervise the construction of physical structures and systems used by the public, including buildings, water supply and sewerage networks, roads and railways, airports, dams, tunnels, sports stadiums, and bridges. Life without civil engineers would be difficult, dangerous, and very uncomfortable.

- There would be no clean tap water because water purification plants would never have been built.
- The environment would suffer because dirty water would not wash away into sewers, to be treated and reused.

Civil engineers not only design public buildings but also make sure they are constructed properly. This massive sports stadium was built for the 2000 Olympic Games in Sydney, Australia.

Dealing with Disaster

After a disaster, such as an earthquake or a hurricane, civil engineers often become as important as doctors. Their help is urgently needed to set up systems that provide clean drinking water and dispose of waste. They are also needed to help guide the safe reconstruction of roads, buildings, and bridges.

- Land transportation would be slow, difficult, and, in some cases, impossible if roads, railroads, and bridges were never constructed.
- Buildings such as airports and railroad stations would not exist, and without them, long-distance national and international transportation systems would never have been developed.
- Sports would never have been organized at professional levels without stadiums, arenas, and sports complexes.
- Without the physical facilities and services that promote public health, deadly diseases would quickly become **epidemics**, killing large numbers of people.

Transportation and energy are very different kinds of public services. Both can benefit, however, from huge concrete dams designed by civil engineers.

Main responsibilities of a civil engineer

Among the broad responsibilities of civil engineers is designing buildings. Civil engineers differ from architects, however, in that their designs focus more on strength, safety, and environmental concerns and less on the artistic aspects of architectural design.

Civil engineering is one of the oldest fields of engineering and has many specialties.

Railroads depend on civil engineers to design efficient railway systems and networks, as well as the buildings and equipment that make up their **infrastructure**.

- **Geotechnical** engineers study the land on which a building will be constructed to make sure the structure will be stable and safe.
- In the field of facilities management, civil engineers examine the places where people work. Their function is to create safe and efficient work environments.

Good Points and Bad Points

"What I like best about my work as a civil engineer is that no two days are ever the same. I also enjoy going out to a work site and seeing the progress on structures being built from my designs."

"Sometimes, the work can be hectic, with several projects demanding my attention at the same time."

- Civil engineers involved with environmental research develop ways to minimize the effects of human activity on the environment, such as designing and installing water recycling systems. They also work to protect plants and animals by investigating environmental damage that could be caused by planned engineering work.
- In transportation, civil engineers improve and rebuild existing roads and bridges and plan, design, and supervise the building of new ones.
- In coastal areas, civil engineers devise ways to protect the land against flooding and **erosion**. They are also involved in building marinas, harbors, canals, and docks.

Other areas of responsibility for civil engineers include:

- working on energy development projects, such as wind farms and power plants
- risk management, which involves assessing the dangers of a project, such as injury to workers or environmental damage, before the project begins
- supervising the construction of large structures, such as skyscrapers, airports, sports stadiums, and housing complexes
- building transportation tunnels through mountains or under rivers or oceans
- doing laboratory research that will lead to improved building materials and techniques

A civil engineer's tasks on a bridge building project might include estimating costs, organizing **contractors**, making sure designs meet government specifications, and overseeing construction and quality control.

Main qualifications of a civil engineer

Good educational background

Anyone wanting to become a civil engineer needs to have studied advanced mathematics, such as calculus and trigonometry; sciences, including biology, physics, and chemistry; social sciences; and computer and information technology.

Computer skills

In some areas of civil engineering, the speed and efficiency of computers have made certain types of design, research, and analysis possible that, previously, were too time-consuming, expensive, or far beyond human abilities to perform. Today's engineers must consider an understanding of computer technology a basic engineering skill.

Creativity

Civil engineers need to be able to visualize how structures should look to best serve the purposes for which they will be built.

Teamwork

The work of civil engineers depends a lot on the work of others. They are usually part of a team and must be skillful in communicating and working closely with others.

Constructing a tunnel beneath the English Channel, to create a better transportation link between England and France, was a huge project for civil engineers. Its construction involved almost 13,000 engineers, technicians, and laborers.

Many of the wonders of the modern world were designed by civil engineers.

Management skills

Civil engineers need to know how to manage projects, including making sure that all the different groups involved in a project have the information they need and keeping the project within a set budget and time frame.

Concern for safety

In design and construction, civil engineers must know how to build structures safely. They must fully understand building methods as well as how construction machinery and equipment works.

fact file

Jobs in civil engineering require at least a four-year bachelor's degree in civil engineering. In the third or fourth year of a degree program, students usually select a specialized field of civil engineering to pursue. More than one-third of the college graduates in civil engineering go on to earn master's degrees, often while working as engineers. To qualify for most jobs, a civil engineer must be a professional engineer (PE) who is licensed in his or her state of employment.

Karen Bridges

Karen is a senior engineer for a consulting company that undertakes projects for clients ranging from construction companies to public works departments. Karen has a bachelor's degree in civil engineering and is a licensed professional engineer.

8:30 a.m.   I'm already hard at work, studying a plan for a building site so I can advise a client on how to move the various construction vehicles onto it.

9:30 a.m.   I attend a team meeting about a project for a new theater. The team is made up of civil engineers from several specialties. Together, we have to decide how to build the theater, what **ecology** needs protection, and how people will travel to the site.

11:00 a.m.   I give a speech to college graduates about the importance of becoming professional engineers.

12:30 p.m.   I receive a phone call from a supervising engineer at a construction site, telling me that a crane is having difficulty moving into position. I review the site plans and offer some suggestions to try to solve the problem.

1:30 p.m.   There's no time for a lunch break today, so I eat a sandwich while I'm putting the final touches on project plans for a recreation center that needs to add an access road for automobile traffic. I had to design the road and calculate the cost. I have a meeting to present my plans to the client in less than an hour.

I work hard. There are new projects on my desk almost every day, but I like the challenge of dealing with several projects at the same time.

2:15 p.m.   I meet with the recreation center client to present my plans and cost estimates for the access road.

3:30 p.m.   I put on a hard hat and protective clothing and visit the site with the crane problem. My solutions worked, and construction is back on schedule.

4:30 p.m.   It's almost time to go home for the day, but I'm excited about the theater project so I grab a cup of coffee and start sketching some site plans.

This civil engineer is a specialist in geotechnical engineering. He's trying to determine when a volcano is likely to erupt. His findings will help protect the people who live near the volcano.

Civil engineers often work on site to make sure buildings are constructed properly.

Electrical Engineer

What is an electrical engineer?

Electrical engineers design, construct, and maintain products and services that use electricity. The field of electrical engineering includes both electrical and electronics engineers. The two jobs sound similar, and, in some ways, they are. Both work closely with electricity, of course, but, at the same time, there are distinct differences between them.

Electrical engineers are concerned mainly with systems that generate electricity and supply it to homes, businesses, schools, hospitals, and factories.

Electronics engineers design and develop electronic devices that use electricity. These products range from computer games to heart monitors.

Some electrical engineers work in the control centers of power companies that supply electricity to millions of people.

What is electricity?

Scientists have long known that electricity exists and how to generate it on a large scale but still find it difficult to explain exactly what electricity is. One explanation is that electricity is a form of energy produced by the movement of **electrons**. Although they may be oversimplifying, some scientists say there are two kinds of electricity: static electricity, such as lightning, which stays in one place, and current electricity, which is an electric charge flowing through a **conductor**. Current electricity is the source of energy in homes and industry.

Both specialties involve research and development, designing new kinds of electrical equipment, and improving existing services and equipment.

Less than one hundred years ago, people would have found it hard to imagine themselves living in houses filled with equipment run by electricity. Yet, today, refrigerators, vacuum cleaners, washing machines, televisions, and computers are found in almost every home. These appliances and devices would not exist, and would not be able to operate, without the knowledge and skills of electrical and electronics engineers.

Large electricity distribution stations like this one supply the electrical power needed in homes and businesses within a certain area or region.

Main responsibilities of an electrical engineer

Electrical engineering includes many specializations, and each specialization has its own responsibilities. Some of the more general responsibilities of electrical engineers include:

- discovering new ways to use energy sources, such as **fossil fuels**, water (hydroelectric energy), the Sun (solar energy), wind, and nuclear power, to produce electricity
- designing equipment to generate and distribute electricity
- determining the demand for electricity in particular areas or regions or the energy needs of particular buildings
- supervising the installation of electrical equipment, such as power lines and **transformers**
- troubleshooting problems with electrical equipment and making sure that all equipment is installed and operated safely

Electricity is delivered by means of **circuits**, which need to be carefully drawn and constructed. This engineer is working on a blueprint of electrical circuits.

Good Points and Bad Points

"Whether you want research, design, installation, or maintenance, electronics engineers have many interesting jobs open to them. The pay is good and so are the opportunities for advancement."

"I feel that electrical engineers need more recognition for their hard work. They provide people with warm homes, good transportation systems, and a great many other comforts and conveniences."

Electronics engineers design, develop, install, and maintain a remarkable range of electrical products in a wide variety of industries, including:

- Communication — Electronics engineers design and develop telecommunication systems that send information through **electromagnetic waves** via satellites. Their knowledge and skills provide us with equipment such as HDTV (high definition television) and cell phones that can send messages, photos, and video clips.

Electronics engineers design and build the robotic arms that are often used by automobile manufacturers.

- Microelectronics — Electronics engineers are behind the technology that is making electrical parts smaller and smaller. The first computer weighed tons, but today, a computer can fit inside a wristwatch. Engineers working in the area of **nanotechnology** design machines that are no bigger than a speck of dust. In the future, these machines might possibly be programmed to travel inside the human body, fighting disease and repairing damage.
- Robotics — Electronics engineers design and build robots and other kinds of **artificial intelligence**, including computers that may, one day, be able to think for themselves.
- Health care — Electronics engineers are vital to the advancement of health care technology. They design and maintain scanning and **ultrasound** equipment, which helps doctors see what is going on inside a patient's body, and electronic sensors, which guide surgeons when they are performing delicate operations.

Main qualifications of an electrical engineer

Mathematics and science background
Education for electrical or electronics engineering should include strong emphasis on high-level math, such as calculus, and on physical sciences, especially physics and chemistry.

Knowledge of computer technology
Computer skills are important qualifications in most fields of engineering but especially in electrical engineering. Besides using computers and **software** to help them do their work, some electrical engineers use computers to actually make computers or contribute in other ways to advancing computer technology. Computers are also used to control most of the facilities that generate power.

An inquiring mind
To understand both why things work a certain way and how to make things work a certain way, electrical and electronics engineers need to be curious and enjoy solving problems and puzzles.

Creative and analytical abilities
Electrical and electronics engineers would not be able to produce the technology and products they do without creativity and analytical ability. These skills help engineers determine what society needs and how best to meet those needs. They also help in defining the steps that must be taken to follow through.

This engineer is adjusting a transformer. Electrical engineers need to be interested in how and why things work the way they do.

Using renewable resources, such as wind, and developing new ways to generate electricity are vital to meeting the energy needs of the future.

Teamwork

Electrical engineers often work in teams, where sharing knowledge, expertise, and ideas is extremely important. They need to work well with colleagues and coworkers and pay attention to the ideas and opinions of other professionals.

Communication skills

Well-developed speaking and writing skills are extremely important. An electrical engineer's instructions and explanations must be clear and understandable, whether the engineer is using technical language for knowledgeable professionals or is simplifying technical information for non-engineers.

fact file

The minimum education requirement for a job as an electrical or electronics engineer is a Bachelor of Science degree. A master's degree is also needed for many design, development, and research positions and helps graduate engineers establish their areas of specialization. Even with their college degrees, however, most electrical engineers spend time, on a regular basis, in formal or informal continuing education.

A day in the life of an electrical engineer

Vivian Lang

Vivian is a senior engineer at an automobile manufacturing company. She has a degree in electrical engineering with a specialization in electronics. Vivian heads a team of ten engineers, working on the research and development of in-car telephones, radios, and navigation equipment.

9:00 a.m. I conduct a team meeting to discuss performance in the customer service aspects of our work. We deal with customer issues as well as designing and developing new equipment. When a customer is dissatisfied with the electrical equipment in his or her car, the problem is passed on to us.

10:30 a.m. I supervise some tests on equipment my team is working on. Testing new equipment is a three-step process. First, we test the equipment on a workbench in the laboratory. Then, we test it on what is known as a breadboard, which is a lab car without a **chassis** or wheels. After these tests have been completed, the equipment is installed in a vehicle, and everything is tested again.

12:30 p.m. Back at my desk, I make some phone calls and check my E-mail messages before going to lunch.

2:00 p.m. I organize my notes and head off to a meeting of company executives. People expect a lot from their cars these days so, at this meeting, we will be looking at ways to better meet customers' needs in the future.

5:00 p.m. A lot of good ideas were brought up at the meeting. I stay a while longer to discuss them informally with some other engineers.

5:30 p.m. Before I call it a day, I spend about half an hour reviewing and scheduling tasks for tomorrow.

Continued advancement in technology means more and more opportunities for electronics engineers. This engineer is examining a **silicon wafer**, which is used in the manufacture of computers.

The computerized dashboard on this expensive new car was built with the help of electronics engineers.

Manufacturing Engineer

What is a manufacturing engineer?

Manufacturing engineers **justify**, plan, design, and coordinate systems and processes that are used to change raw materials into manufactured goods. Their work includes every aspect of manufacturing, sometimes even helping with product design, and they are often involved in several different types of engineering, especially mechanical, electrical, and industrial engineering.

What do cars, cans, and cookies all have in common? The answer is that none of these products would exist without manufacturing engineers. Jobs in this field of engineering can be found in industries ranging from automobiles and agricultural equipment to foods and **pharmaceuticals**.

Although their work also includes duties such as analyzing **data** and writing reports, most manufacturing engineers spend only part of their workdays sitting at desks. They are typically found in production areas, where

An ice cream production plant uses big machines that have lots of moving parts. Manufacturing engineers make sure the machines run smoothly.

The Canning Process

In 1795, Emperor Napoleon of France offered a prize to the person who could think of the best way of preserving food for the French army. An inventor named Nicholas Appert came up with the idea for a canning process. Canning quickly became one of the world's largest manufacturing industries. Today, almost every home has some kind of canned food on kitchen shelves.

goods are being made, listening to the people who operate the machines and making sure all machinery is working properly.

Manufacturing engineers are always looking for ways to improve production, such as:

- figuring out how to make processing systems and operators more efficient
- improving the quality of products
- finding new methods to reduce production costs
- keeping work areas and production processes and equipment as safe as possible

A manufacturing engineer in a pharmaceutical factory must maintain a germ-free environment.

Main responsibilities of a manufacturing engineer

Among the main responsibilities of manufacturing engineers are designing or purchasing production equipment and planning its uses. Machinery is a big investment so, before any money is spent, engineers must do a lot of research to make sure companies buy or build the best possible equipment for their needs. The most basic part of this research is answering the following questions.

- What job or jobs will the machinery do?
- How will the new machinery fit in with existing machinery?
- How much money is available for new equipment?
- Will the equipment justify its cost?
- When is the equipment needed?

Beyond research, a manufacturing engineer's responsibilities usually include:

- writing justification reports, which explain research methods and findings on recommended equipment

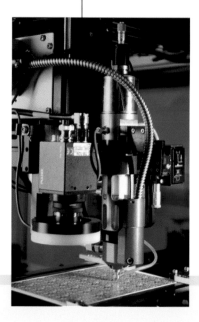

Automated equipment, such as this machine for assembling computer chips, is very expensive. Manufacturing engineers need to make sure that costly equipment is correctly installed and used efficiently.

Good Points and Bad Points

"I get a lot of satisfaction from running an efficient production area and knowing that I play an important role in the company's success."

"Sometimes, people expect me to be able to work miracles, asking me, for example, to repair a machine or install new equipment in an impossibly short period of time."

- buying equipment and adapting it to meet the company's manufacturing needs
- designing new equipment to suit company needs and supervising the construction of the designs
- installing and testing new machines and equipment (Each piece of equipment has to work well with all of the other machinery in a manufacturing system.)
- organizing operator training on new equipment
- performing regular maintenance checks to make sure that equipment is running smoothly and safely
- identifying and correcting production system problems (Even in the most efficiently run factories, machinery breaks down. Breakdowns are usually very expensive, and companies stand to lose a lot of money when goods are not being produced. Engineers must see that problems are corrected as quickly as possible.)

Manufacturing engineers are trained to work with complex production machinery. This engineer is working on machinery in a factory that manufactures **hydraulic** test equipment.

Main qualifications of a manufacturing engineer

A diverse educational background

Manufacturing is a complex process that requires a wide range of knowledge and skills. For all engineers, a background in math, science, and the basic principles of engineering is essential, but manufacturing engineers also need to have specialized knowledge of materials, energy, manufacturing processes, and mechanical/electrical systems.

Practical skills

Besides understanding how machinery and production systems operate, manufacturing engineers have to be able to work in a hands-on way with factory equipment. Especially in this field of engineering, the desire and ability to take machinery apart and figure out exactly how it works can be very useful.

To deal effectively with production and assembly line problems, a manufacturing engineer must be a clear and careful communicator.

Computer skills

Engineers use computers for many tasks, from designing machinery to storing information and writing reports. Besides using computers for research and development, manufacturing engineers use computer technology to control production processes and equipment.

Problem-solving skills

On the job, manufacturing engineers often find that problem-solving skills can be more valuable than what they learned in classrooms. Many of the problems they encounter do not have clear-cut solutions, so engineers must rely on intuitive, creative, and listening abilities.

The bottled water on this **conveyor belt** will soon be for sale on store shelves.

fact file

The minimum requirement to be a manufacturing engineer is a bachelor's degree in that field, but because few U. S. colleges offer this program, a bachelor's degree in mechanical or industrial engineering, along with hands-on manufacturing experience, is one of several commonly accepted alternatives.

Teamwork

Any manufacturing process is a team effort. Engineers need to enjoy being part of a team and know how to be effective team builders and leaders.

Communication skills

Developing good speaking, writing, and listening skills is essential. Manufacturing engineers must be able to interact effectively with machine operators, materials suppliers, company managers, maintenance personnel, and customers. Most importantly, engineers must be able to explain technical matters to people who do not have technical knowledge or backgrounds.

High safety standards

Factories can be dangerous places, and manufacturing engineers need to develop and promote cautious and careful processes and practices.

Matthew Clubb

Matthew works as a manufacturing engineer for a small company that makes tools for use in large-scale drilling operations around the world.

9:00 a.m. My first major task of the day is putting together a price quote for a drilling tool to be used on an offshore oil **rig**. A price quote involves finding out the cost of the different manufacturing materials and estimating the number of hours it will take to make the tool. Coming up with accurate and reasonable price quotes is very tricky, and I can't afford to make a mistake.

11:00 a.m. I'm at my computer, now, designing some tools requested by another client in the oil industry. I'm using **CAD software** to create **three-dimensional** drawings of my designs on screen. Drilling tool designs are very detailed and have to be correct down to thousandths of an inch.

1:00 p.m. Lunch is just a sandwich and a cup of coffee, eaten at my desk.

2:00 p.m. The tool designs are ready for our client to review. For quick delivery, I send them over the Internet, through a password-protected system that only the client can access.

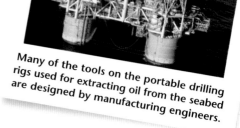

Many of the tools on the portable drilling rigs used for extracting oil from the seabed are designed by manufacturing engineers.

To solve production problems and make sure jobs are completed on time, manufacturing engineers sometimes have to put their practical skills, such as **welding**, to use in the machine shop.

3:00 p.m.   I'm hard at work, planning some manufacturing processes for upcoming projects, when a phone call comes through about the designs I sent out a short time ago. Eager to keep the project on track, the client has already reviewed the designs and is calling to talk over some desired changes.

3:30 p.m.   I'm in the machine shop, talking to one of the operators who turns my designs into reality. Five operators work here, and we all stay in close contact to make sure manufacturing, from design to product delivery, runs smoothly and successfully.

5:00 p.m.   Everything is on schedule today, so we can shut down for the night. There have been times when all of us have worked late and through weekends in the machine shop to finish a job on time.

Marine Engineer

What is a marine engineer?

Marine engineers design, build, and operate ships and other watercraft, from tugboats to oil tankers and sailboats to submarines. Although commonly referred to as marine engineering, this field actually consists of three interrelated professions: naval architecture, marine engineering, and ocean engineering. Each profession, in its own way, makes possible the use of the seas and oceans that cover 70 percent of Earth's surface.

Ocean engineers design underwater scooters and other small craft for deepsea exploration.

Naval architects mainly design ships and other watercraft. Besides determining the basic size, shape, and structure of vessels, this type of engineer is also responsible for power requirements, weight distribution, **hull resistance**, and overall performance and stability.

Built to Be Unsinkable

In 1912, the *Titanic* was the largest ship ever built, and because its hull had sixteen water-tight compartments, engineers thought it was unsinkable. The walls of the compartments had doors that could be closed if a compartment began to fill with water. The walls, however, did not reach to the ceiling, so water overflowed from one compartment to the next. After hitting an iceberg on its first voyage, the *Titanic* sank.

Marine engineers work mostly with the machinery on ships and watercraft. They design the mechanical, electrical, and control systems that run the vessels. They also select and install related equipment, such as engines, **turbines**, gears, and propellers. Some marine engineers work on board ships, operating and maintaining mechanical systems.

Oceans have been important to world trade for hundreds of years. About 98 percent of all international cargo is shipped by sea.

Ocean engineers work with the ocean environment in many different ways, including studying ocean movement and its effects on watercraft. Part of their work, too, is designing and developing instruments and vehicles able to explore areas of the ocean that were previously out of human reach.

Main responsibilities of a marine engineer

Naval architect

The work of designing and constructing seaworthy watercraft, including cargo ships, passenger liners, submarines, ferries, tugboats, yachts, and tankers, typically includes the following tasks:

- meeting with a client to develop the design of a vessel
- determining the best materials to use, such as steel, wood, aluminum, or fiberglass
- estimating construction costs
- supervising construction

Whether a marine engineer works on a ship or onshore, a laptop computer is a valuable tool for calculations, reports, and record keeping.

Marine engineer

Besides designing, selecting, and installing machinery and equipment on watercraft, a marine engineer may also operate, maintain, or repair equipment, working in an onboard position, such as in an engine room.

Good Points and Bad Points

"I am a marine engineer who works on board a ship. Spending so much time at sea has given me many opportunities to visit different parts of the world. It has also helped me become very independent, which is important because I'm the only engineer on the ship."

"Being away from my family and friends for months at a time was difficult to get used to. I still find myself feeling homesick, sometimes, especially on my birthday and at Christmas."

The tasks of onboard engineers can also include:

- analyzing data and readings from machinery to identify and carry out appropriate adjustments to equipment or operating procedures
- maintaining supplies of equipment and parts
- making sure that the vessel is not causing pollution
- overseeing major maintenance work when the ship or boat is in port or on dry land

Ocean engineer

This heavily environment-related field of engineering focuses on ways to use ocean resources safely and efficiently. Its broad scope includes:

- marine transportation, from designing ports and harbors to planning uses for waterways
- oil and gas production, from exploring undersea petroleum sources to building offshore drilling **rigs**
- conservation, from protecting marine species to preserving world food supplies
- naval defense, from building warships to designing navigation and underwater communication systems

Main qualifications of a marine engineer

Love of the sea

Marine engineers need to have an ongoing fascination for and interest in the sea. Because changes occur so frequently and quickly, they also must be able to keep up with developments, throughout the world, in the fields of science and technology as well as in engineering.

Broad educational background

A solid core of high-level mathematics and sciences, especially physics and chemistry, thorough knowledge of basic engineering principles, and a good understanding of computer technology are essential for any profession in the field of marine engineering. Depending on the profession, knowledge of economics, social studies, or the environment may also be required.

French marine engineer Alain Thébault built this watercraft with wings, called a **hydrofoil**. At high speeds, the hull of this **aerodynamic** craft rises above the water.

Communication skills

Delivering successful oral presentations and writing formal reports require well-developed communication skills. Even foreign language skills may be necessary for marine engineers who want to work in foreign countries or with international teams.

Attention to details

Seas, oceans, and any other large bodies of water are unpredictable and dangerous environments. Whether designing watercraft or operating machinery, even the smallest details can be significant. Marine engineers must work with precision and accuracy and always be as much concerned with safety as with efficiency.

Teamwork

Except, perhaps, for naval architects, who frequently design and build smaller vessels on their own, marine engineering projects usually involve working with a group. Marine engineers need to be able to work well with all kinds of people from a wide variety of educational, and even cultural, backgrounds. Teams can include engineers from many different fields; scientists, such as marine biologists, oceanographers, and geologists; and divers.

fact file

Marine engineering jobs usually require at least a bachelor's degree in naval architecture or marine engineering. At some schools, these courses of study are combined. A degree in ocean engineering is also acceptable for certain kinds of positions. For many jobs, marine engineers may be expected to have work experience or advanced degrees.

Marine engineers who are qualified divers can take advantage of job opportunities involving under-sea exploration.

A day in the life of a marine engineer

Anna Evangelidis

Anna is a marine engineer with an offshore pipeline construction company. She currently works on a ship that is laying pipes to transport oil and gas from the North Sea.

6:30 a.m. My workday starts early. I work a twelve-hour shift, from 7:00 a.m. to 7:00 p.m., seven days a week. For this project, engineers spend six weeks at a time at sea. I'm one of two marine engineers now on board. We started about a month ago.

7:15 a.m. I'm supervising the laying of the pipeline, which is my primary job. I have to make sure each pipe falls into precisely the right place.

Sections of pipe are welded together on board ship, forming a kind of long sausage. Then the length of pipes is dropped into the sea. Computer calculations help me know exactly how and where the pipe has to be dropped to get it in the right position. Divers, who work from a special boat called a dive support vessel, attach the pipe to the offshore platform.

9:30 a.m. We stop to eat.

10:00 a.m. I'm back working already. Time is money so we can't afford long breaks.

Marine engineers can spend weeks or months at a time working on ships at sea.

This marine engineer is running a test on submarine equipment.

2:00 p.m. Everything has been going well until now. The welders are having equipment problems. If the **welding** is not done correctly and does not meet specific standards, it is likely to crack, and oil will leak into the ocean.

We need to lay a set length of pipe each day, but with this unexpected delay, it looks as though we won't meet our target today. The welders on board are skilled workers who know their jobs, so all I can do is wait until they find the problem and resolve it.

3:30 p.m. Tests show that the welding equipment problems have been corrected. We get back to work and try to make up for lost time.

7:00 p.m. I'm done for the day. I often stop at the onboard gym after work, but today, I'm too tired. I'm just going to shower, eat, and go to bed.

Mechanical Engineer

What is a mechanical engineer?

Mechanical engineers work with anything that moves in a mechanical way. They also work with substances that can be moved mechanically, such as air, oil, and water. Basically, any object that is manufactured will have a mechanical engineer involved in its development.

The work of mechanical engineers is divided into a number of specialties and can often overlap with other fields of engineering.

Some mechanical engineers design and develop the gears, pulleys, and other moving parts of engines.

- Medical engineering uses principles of mechanical engineering to design, develop, and test equipment that can improve human health.

Building Up Steam

Although Scottish mechanical engineer and inventor James Watt usually gets the credit for building the first steam engine, it was Thomas Newcomen who actually invented the steam engine, in 1712, before Watt was even born. Used mainly in mines, where it was able to drain water from underground tunnels at much deeper levels than ever before possible, Newcomen's steam engine increased the amount of coal and iron that could be mined.

- **Automotive** engineering involves the design and development of land-based, motorized vehicles, such as cars, trucks, and motorcycles.
- Sports engineering deals with research and design to produce equipment used by athletes.
- Energy engineering involves mechanical, electrical, civil, and chemical engineers, working together to find new ways of converting renewable energy sources, such as wind, water, and sunlight, into electricity for homes and businesses.
- Sales engineering ensures that customers who need mechanical equipment have access to product experts who can help them purchase equipment that suits their needs, monitor product availability, help them make the best use of the products they buy, and assist them if something goes wrong. Often, sales engineers are also included in product design.

The steam engine designed by James Watt (1736–1819) was a great improvement over Thomas Newcomen's steam engine.

Main responsibilities of a mechanical engineer

The work of mechanical engineers can include any of the following areas of responsibility:

- design — deciding how a machine needs to work and drawing up plans to achieve that performance
- development — making plans and designs a reality by building the machine
- testing — running a machine under a variety of conditions to discover and correct problems
- installation — putting a machine in place at a factory or in the environment where it will be used and making sure the machine operates successfully
- operation — monitoring a machine's performance to make sure the machine is working properly
- maintenance and repair — keeping a machine in good working order by identifying the causes of problems that occur and by supervising maintenance staff in correcting the problems

This medical engineer is working on the development of a new type of **syringe**.

Good Points and Bad Points

"I have always wanted a job that holds my attention and keeps me on my toes. The research I do as a medical equipment engineer is both interesting and exciting, and nothing beats the feeling of satisfaction that comes from successfully completing a project. At times, however, the work is painstaking, and there are long periods when, despite my best efforts, I don't seem to be making much progress."

Specific tasks in these areas of responsibility vary for different fields of mechanical engineering. Medical engineering, for example, involves tasks such as designing **prostheses** that are comfortable and can hold onto objects and developing mechanical hearts and **diagnostic** equipment, such as **ultrasound** and X-ray machines. Some medical engineers work on

designing and developing nanorobots that can travel through the human body and repair damaged **arteries**.

The work of automotive engineers includes developing environmentally friendly engines that can run on **alternative fuels**, improving safety equipment such as seat belts and air bags, designing better security systems, and finding ways to prevent **corrosion**.

Sports engineers design, develop, and test equipment used by athletes, such as training shoes that can measure the slipperiness of the ground beneath them.

Examining the technology behind snowboards, skis, and skateboards helps sports engineers design better equipment for athletes.

Main qualifications of a mechanical engineer

Math and science background

The requirements for admission to an engineering school or program include a strong background in math and science, and, in at least their first two years of study, engineering students are required to take additional course work in math and science.

Computer skills

Proficiency with computers is important in many aspects of engineering. For mechanical engineers, it is especially valuable in designing and developing machinery and related equipment.

Computer-aided design (**CAD**) gives mechanical engineers the ability to change their plans and designs quickly and easily.

Problem-solving ability

A main focus of mechanical engineering is finding ways to solve problems with machinery. Mechanical engineers not only have to come up with solutions to problems but also must decide which solutions will work best.

Creativity

Mechanical engineers need to be able to imagine how a machine is going to work and envision the different ways in which the machine could be built.

These mechanical engineers are inspecting a generator at a power plant.

Organized work habits

An organized approach to a project is important because a mechanical engineer must usually work within set budgets and deadlines.

Communication skills

Good communication skills are essential. Engineers must be able to share information, clearly and accurately, both verbally and in writing, with other engineers as well as with clients, coworkers, and specialists in other fields who have little, if any, engineering knowledge.

fact file

Jobs in mechanical engineering require a college degree in mechanical engineering and, in most cases, a graduate must be a licensed Professional Engineer (PE), which requires four years of work experience in engineering and passing a state examination. Because mechanical engineering is used in so many different industries, students often go to graduate school to qualify for a specialization.

Peter Davis

Peter works as a mechanical engineer for a car production company, where he designs exterior trim parts for cars.

9:00 a.m. I'm using a CAD program to work on new body trim for a sports car my company is planning to launch. As I work on a design, I have to keep a lot of information in mind, including the overall look of the car.

I've been fascinated by cars since I was a child, so being part of an automotive design team is about as exciting as it gets for me. My job involves designing parts that are attached to the exterior of a car. These parts include bumpers, **spoilers**, and body side moldings.

11:00 a.m. I attend a meeting to learn the details of a new project — the possible launch of a family car with a sports car look. This project sounds so exciting that the meeting extends right through lunch. We all want to talk about ideas for the new design.

1:45 p.m. Back to reality, I'm running some tests on bumpers I've designed.

Computers are used widely in most areas of car design and production.

These tests are to make sure that the bumpers are strong enough to protect the body of the car. Although the results of the tests seem to be good, I still have to do a lot more testing before I can be completely confident that my designs are ready for production.

3:30 p.m. I start doing a detailed analysis of the results of the bumper tests. Next, I'll have to prepare reports on the analysis, which means putting in about three more hours of work today.

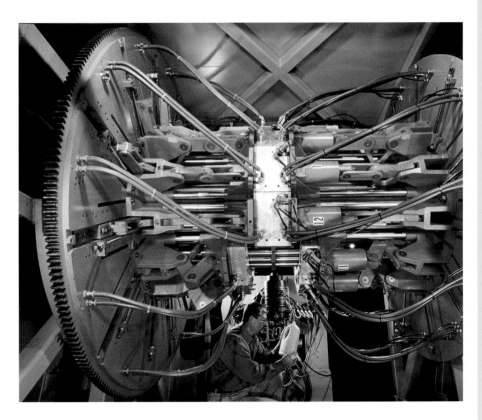

Some mechanical engineers run, or supervise, regular maintenance checks on machinery. In this photo, an engineer is inspecting a huge machine in a plastics processing plant.

Glossary

aerodynamics – the study of how objects move through air

airframe – the outside structure, or body, of an aircraft

alternative fuels – energy-producing materials such as electricity, natural gas, and grain alcohols, which can be burned as fuels but, unlike gasoline, are not made from petroleum or oil

altitude – the measurement of height above ground level

arteries – branching, tubelike vessels inside the bodies of humans and other animals, which carry blood from the heart to other parts of the body

artificial intelligence – machines that can imitate human behaviors and thought processes

automated – operated by means of mechanical or electronic devices instead of human workers

automotive – having to do with motor vehicles, such as automobiles and trucks

CAD – short for "computer-aided design," which is a system of hardware and software that allows engineers to create and manipulate design drawings and specifications on computer screens

chassis – the frame that supports the body and engine of a motor vehicle

circuits – the paths followed by electric currents from their sources of energy to wires or other output devices

conductor – a material or substance that electricity can flow through easily

contractors – people who provide labor, skills, or supplies for the prices and periods of time specified and agreed to by signing contracts

conveyor belt – a mechanical device that carries materials from one place to another on a continuously moving belt

corrosion – a gradual chemical action that destroys metal, such as rusting iron

data – facts or items of information used in planning and calculating

diagnostic – having to do with the diagnosis, or identification, of an illness or medical condition

ecology – the science or study of relationships between living things and their environments

electromagnetic waves – the unseen movement of electric and magnetic forces traveling together through space

electrons – the smallest of the three kinds of electrically charged particles that make up an atom. Electrons have a negative electrical charge.

epidemics – outbreaks of diseases that spread quickly among groups of people

erosion – the wearing away of rock or soil by the action of wind or water

flight control systems – the instruments and connecting mechanisms that control aircraft in flight

fossil fuels – energy-producing materials such as petroleum and coal, formed by the remains of plants and animals that lived millions of years earlier

geotechnical – having to do with the use of geology to help solve certain kinds of engineering problems

hull – the main body of a ship

hydraulic – moved or operated by water pressure

hydrofoil – a boat with fins on the bottom that can lift the hull completely above the water for added speed

infrastructure – all of the buildings, equipment, and other resources needed to operate a system or an organization

internship – a period of training and practice to learn a profession on the job

justify – to prove that something is right or reasonable

nanotechnology – the art and science of using atoms or molecules of materials to develop microscopic devices

pharmaceuticals – drugs and other types of medicines

propulsion – the means by which an object is pushed forward

prostheses – manufactured, artificial body parts

resistance – an opposing force that slows down speed or movement

rig – machinery that is set up and equipped for a specific use

silicon wafer – a thin slice of silicon, needed to build the semiconductors and microchips used in computers, televisions, and other electronic and telecommunication devices

simulation – an electronic imitation of an actual event, situation, or process, which is often used for training purposes

software – computer programs that supply the instructions for performing specific electronic functions

spoilers – air deflectors that help keep fast-moving automobiles from rising off the road

synthetics – materials that are made, or manufactured, from chemicals

syringe – an instrument used to inject or withdraw fluids

tank wagons – road vehicles that carry large tanks, which can be loaded and unloaded without removing the tanks

teleconference – a meeting of people at two or more locations, making contact through telecommunication equipment, such as phones and video links

three-dimensional – having height, width, and depth

transformers – machines that change the voltage of electric current

turbines – types of engines, which have curved blades, or vanes, attached to a central drive shaft that is turned by the pushing force of steam, air, or water pressing against the blades

ultrasound – a diagnostic procedure that uses high-frequency vibrations to create a two-dimensional image of internal body structures

welding – using heat, usually from a flame, to join pieces of metal or plastic

Further Information

This book does not cover all engineering jobs. Many are not mentioned, including agricultural engineer and environmental engineer. This book does, however, give you an idea of the range of engineering careers and what working in engineering is like.

Engineering is a practical profession with many opportunities to make valuable contributions. Today's engineers are increasingly involved in projects and positions that require combinations of engineering skills. The fields of mechanical and electrical engineering, for example, overlap in projects involving electronic equipment that has mechanical parts. Because this trend is likely to continue, many of tomorrow's engineers will need skills in more than one kind of engineering.

The only way to decide if working in engineering is right for you is to find out what this kind of work involves. Read as much as you can about engineering careers and talk to people, especially people you know, who work in engineering.

When you are in middle school or high school, a teacher or career counselor might be able to help you arrange some work experience in an engineering profession. After high school, if you are still considering a career in engineering, choose the subjects you will study in college with care, making sure they meet requirements for your preferred engineering career.

Books

Careers in Focus: Engineering
(Ferguson, 2003)

Cool Careers for Girls in Engineering
Ceel Pasternak and Linda Thornburg
(Sagebrush, 2001)

I Want to Be . . . an Engineer
Stephanie Maze and Catherine O'Neill Grace
(Harcourt, 1999)

Women in Engineering Careers
Jetty Kahn
(Capstone Press, 1999)

Web Sites

The Civil Engineer
www.careers.iptv.org/ enhanced/1055/ ec_careerhome.cfm

Discover Engineering
www.discoverengineering. org

Engineering and You
www.nspe.org/students/ st1-cfy.asp

Ocean Engineering
www.marinecareers.net/ oceaneng.htm

Useful Addresses

Aerospace Engineer

American Institute of Aeronautics
and Astronautics, Inc.
1801 Alexander Bell Drive, Suite 500
Reston, VA 20191-4344
Tel: (703) 264-7500 (800) 639-2422
www.aiaa.org/content.cfm?pageid=214

Aerospace Industries Association
1000 Wilson Boulevard, Suite 1700
Arlington, VA 22209-3901
Tel: (703) 359-1000
www.aia-aerospace.org

Chemical Engineer

American Institute of Chemical
Engineers (AIChE)
3 Park Avenue
New York, NY 10016-5991
Tel: (212) 591-7096 (800) 242-4363
www.aiche.org

American Chemical Society
Department of Career Services
1155 16th Street NW
Washington, DC 20036
Tel: (800) 227-5558
www.chemistry.org

Civil Engineer

American Society of Civil Engineers
1801 Alexander Bell Drive
Reston, VA 20191-4400
Tel: (800) 548-2723
www.asce.org

Electrical Engineer

Institute of Electrical and Electronics
Engineers (IEEE), Inc.
445 Hoes Lane
Piscataway, NJ 08854-1331
Tel: (732) 981-0060
www.ieee.com

Manufacturing Engineer

Society of Manufacturing Engineers
International Headquarters
One SME Drive
P. O. Box 930
Dearborn, MI 48121
Tel: (800) 733-4763
www.sme.org
www.manufacturingiscool.com

Marine Engineer

The Society of Naval Architects
and Marine Engineers
601 Pavonia Avenue
Jersey City, NJ 07306
Tel: (201) 798-4800 (800) 798-2188
www.sname.org

Mechanical Engineer

The American Society of Mechanical
Engineers (ASME International)
3 Park Avenue
New York, NY 10016-5990
Tel: (212) 591-7722 (800) 843-2763
www.asme.org

Index